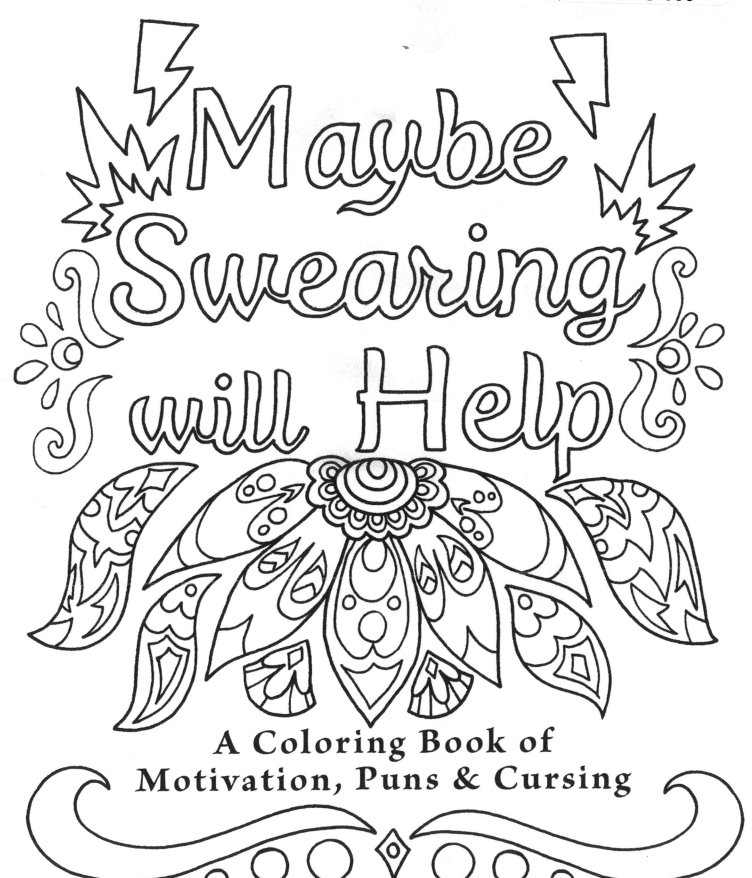

Maybe Swearing will Help

A Coloring Book of Motivation, Puns & Cursing

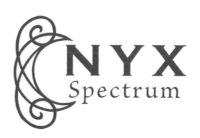

Published in 2016 by
Nyx Spectrum

ISBN: 9780996764131

Printed in the United States of America

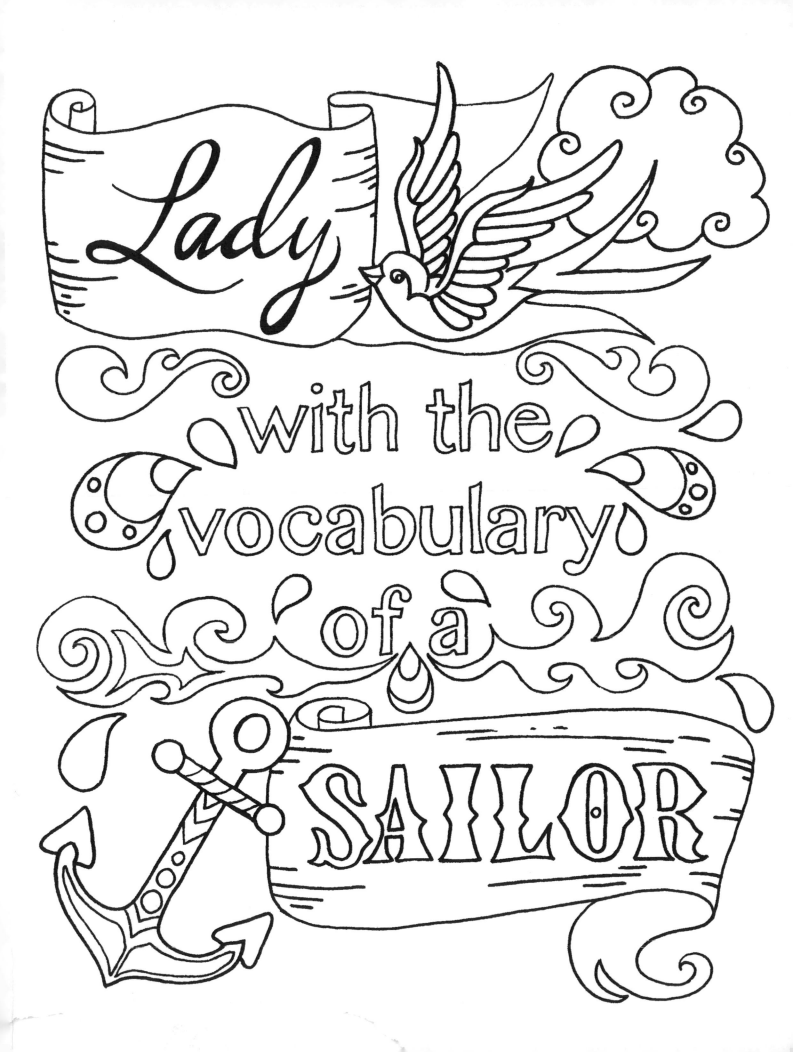

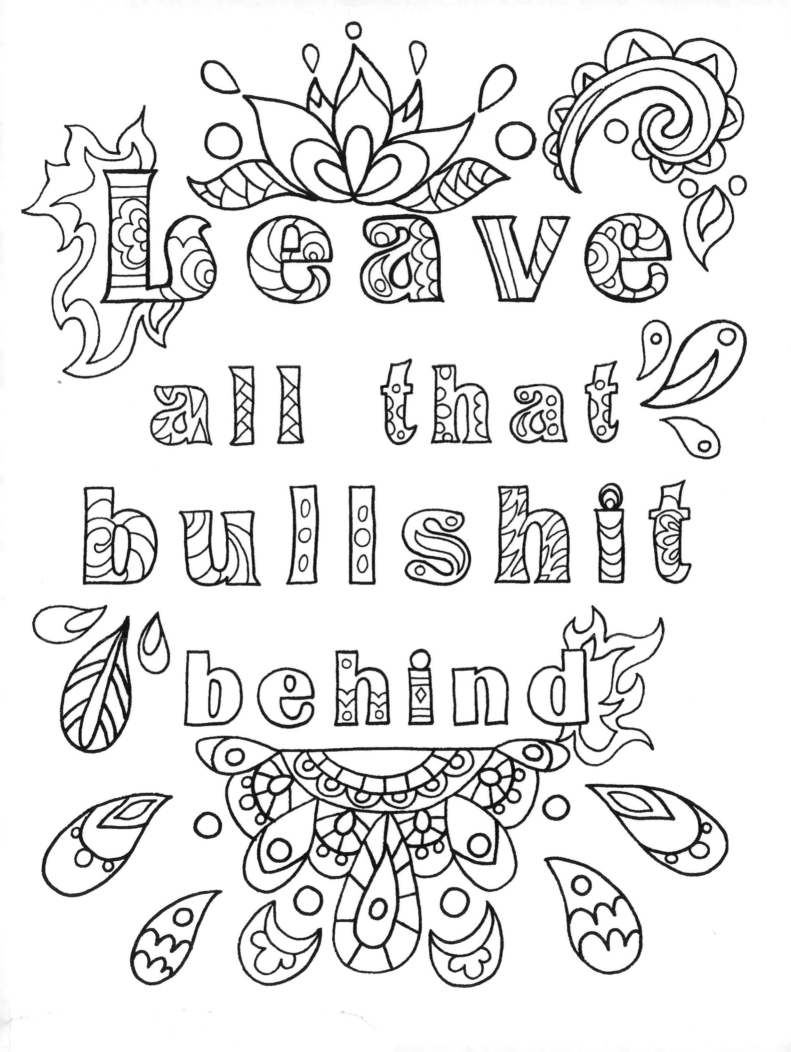

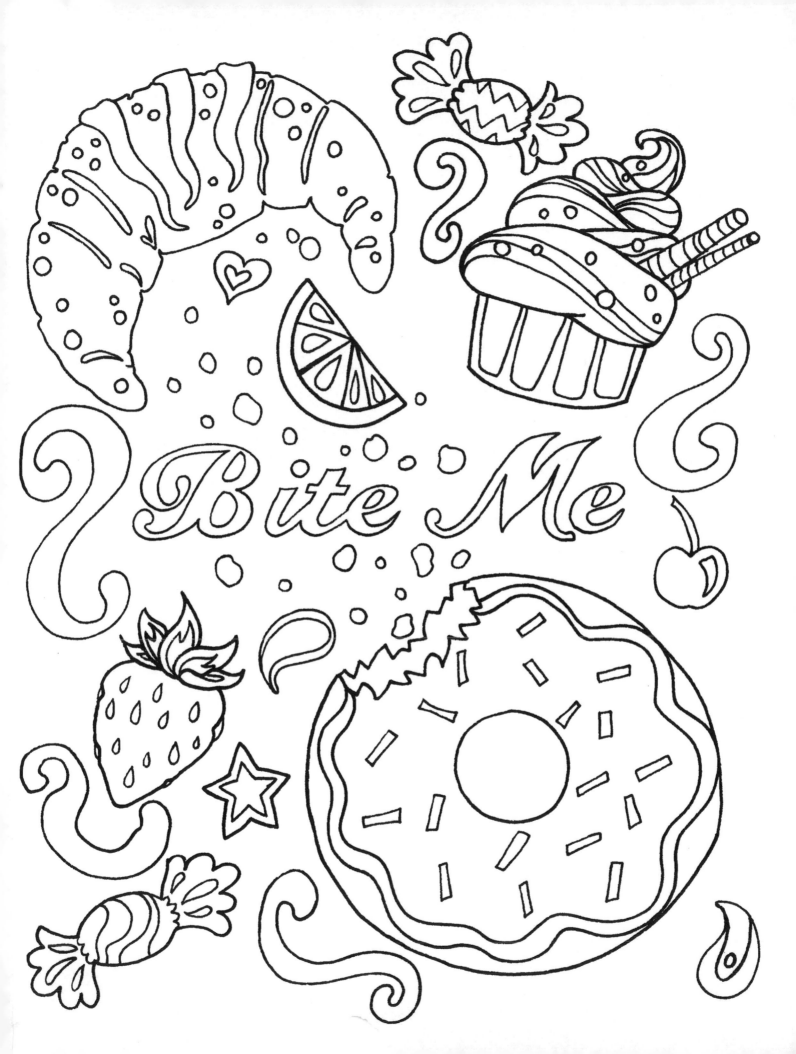

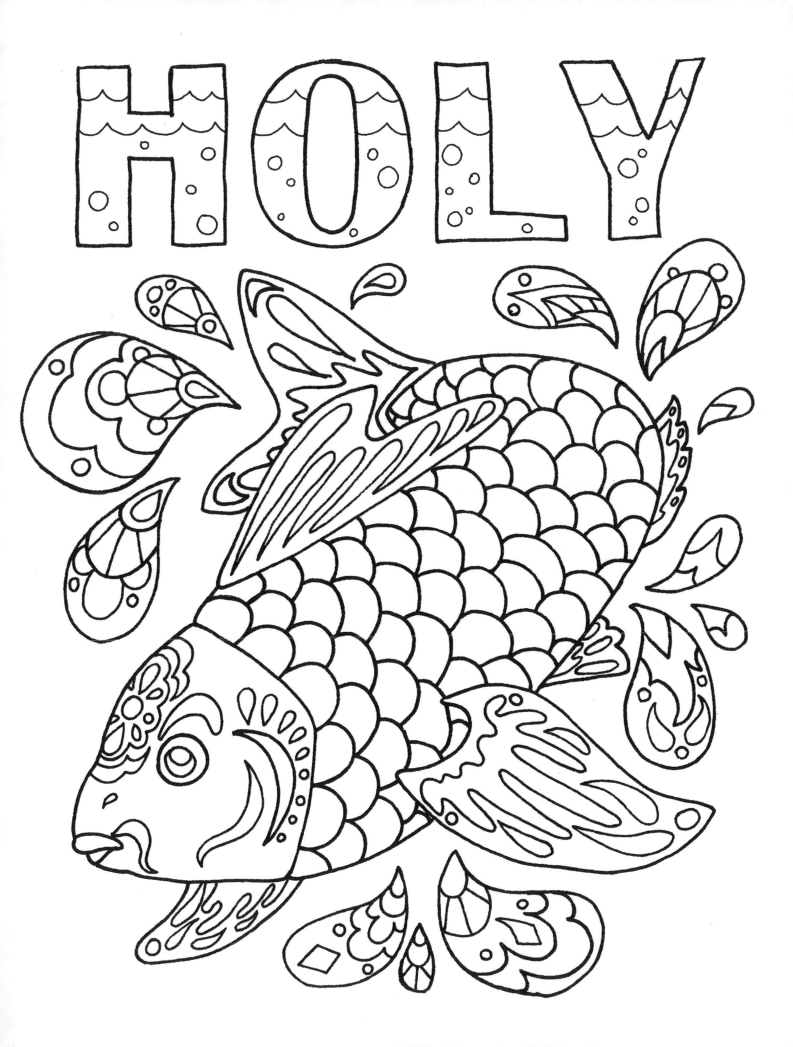

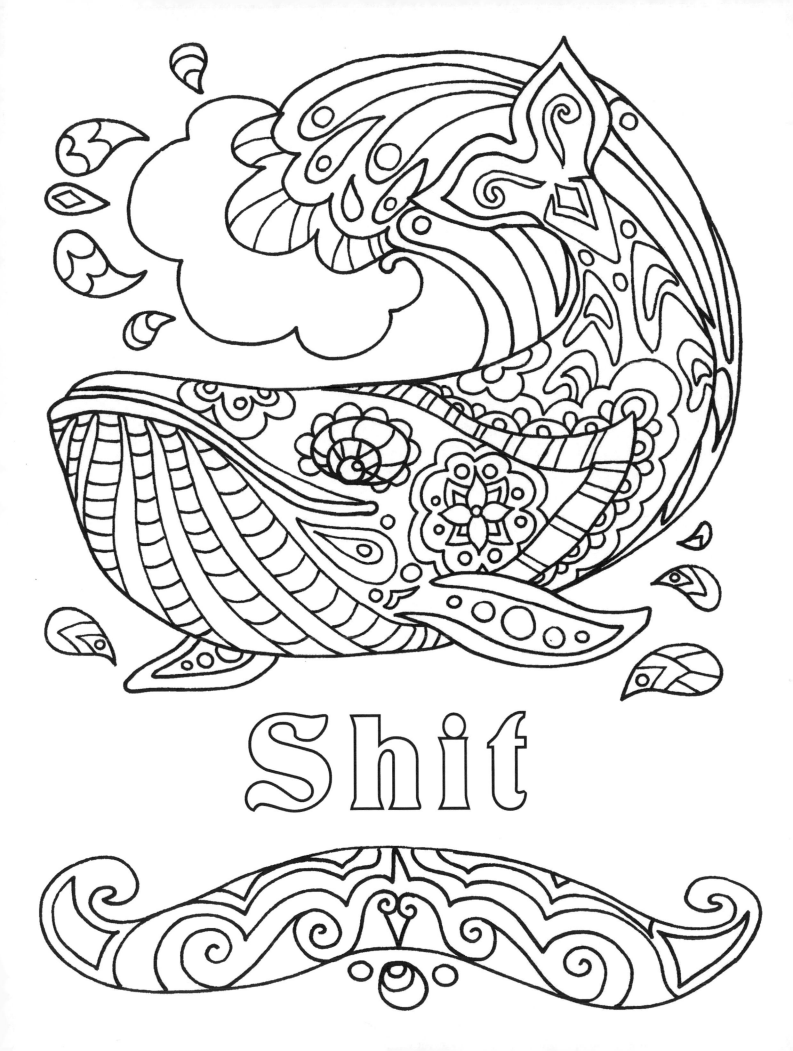

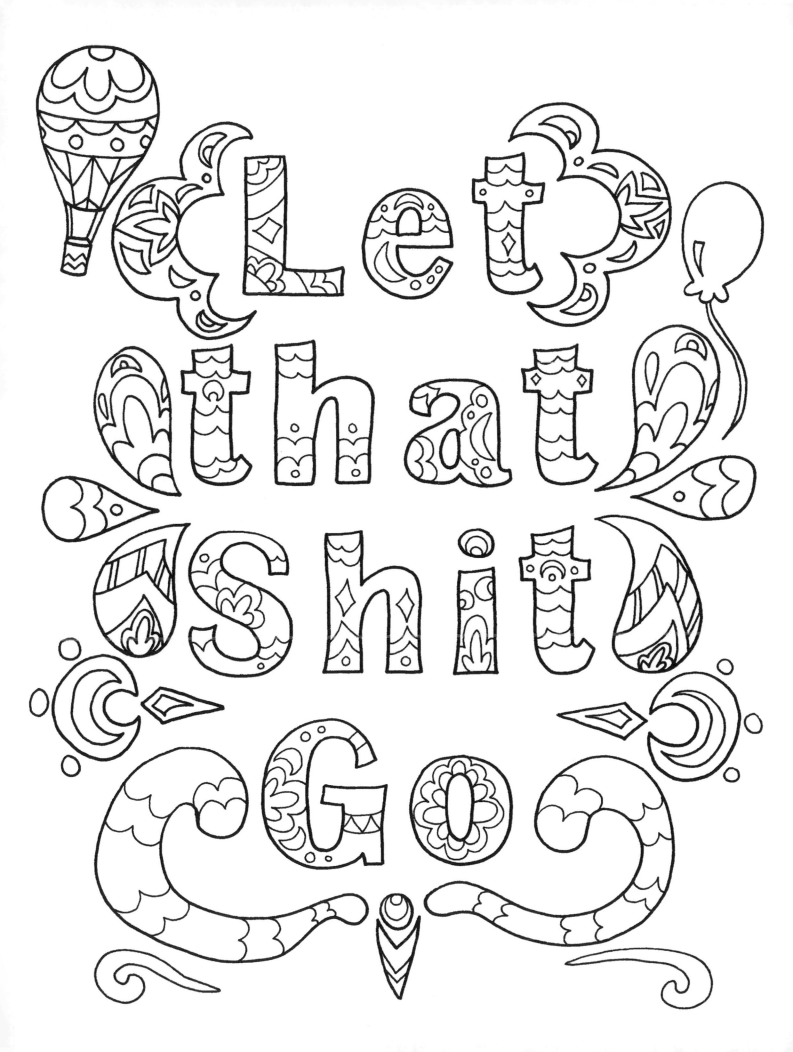

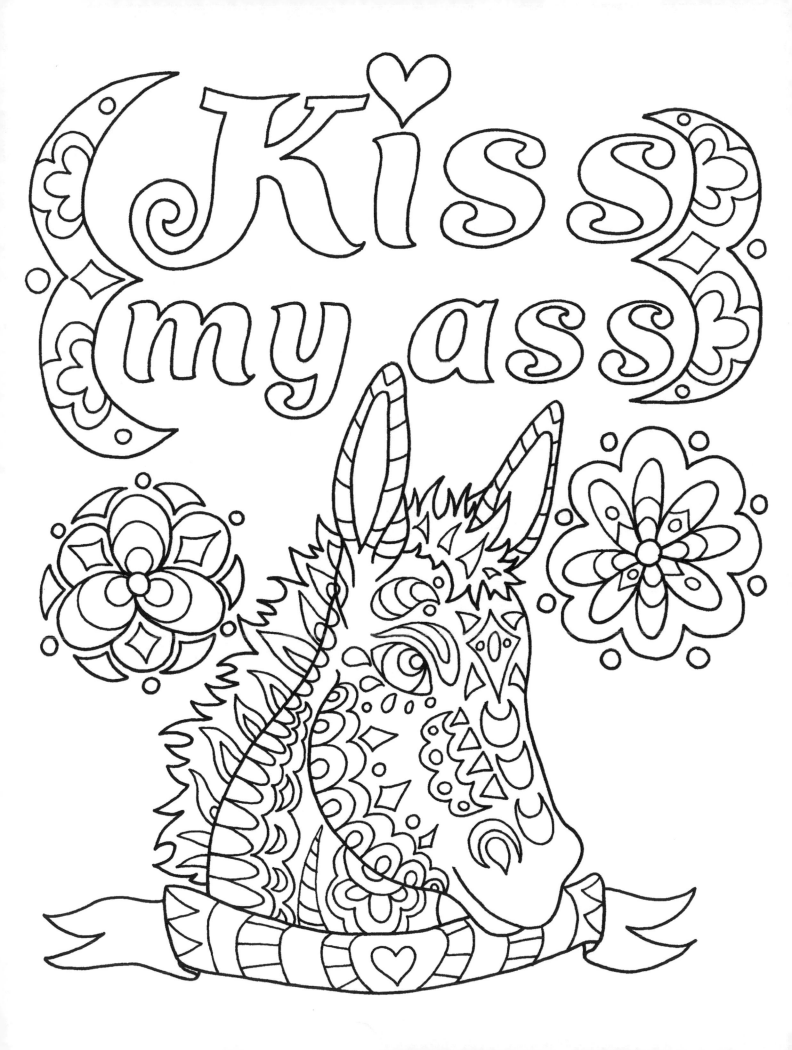

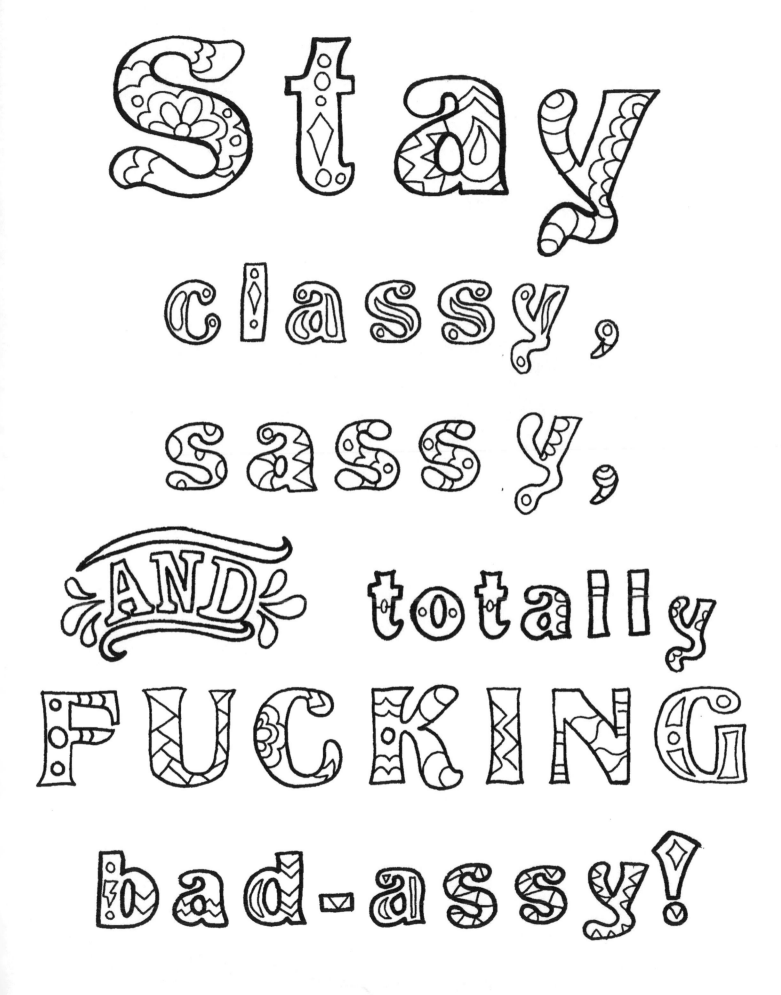

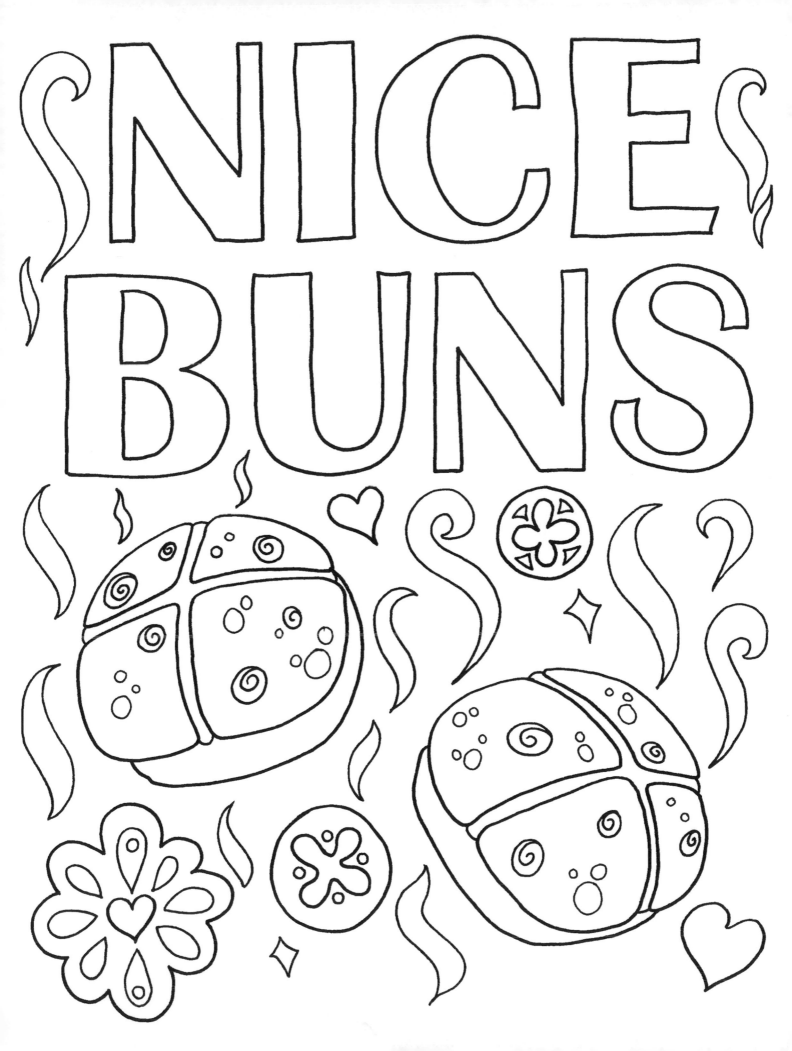

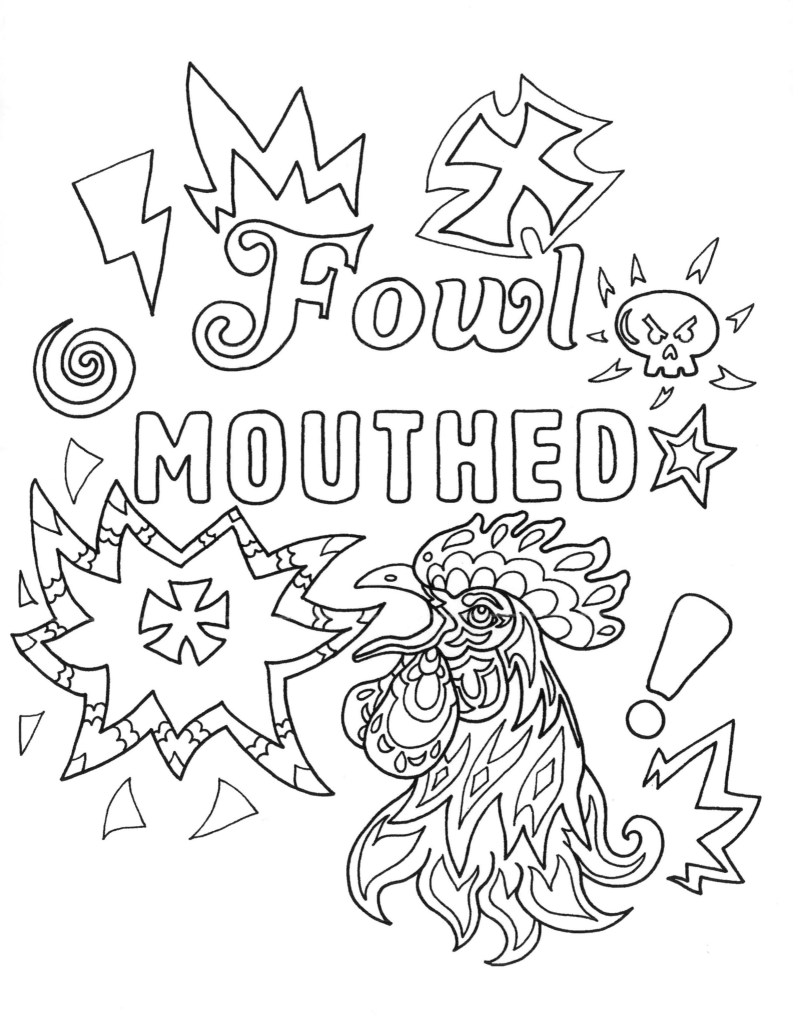

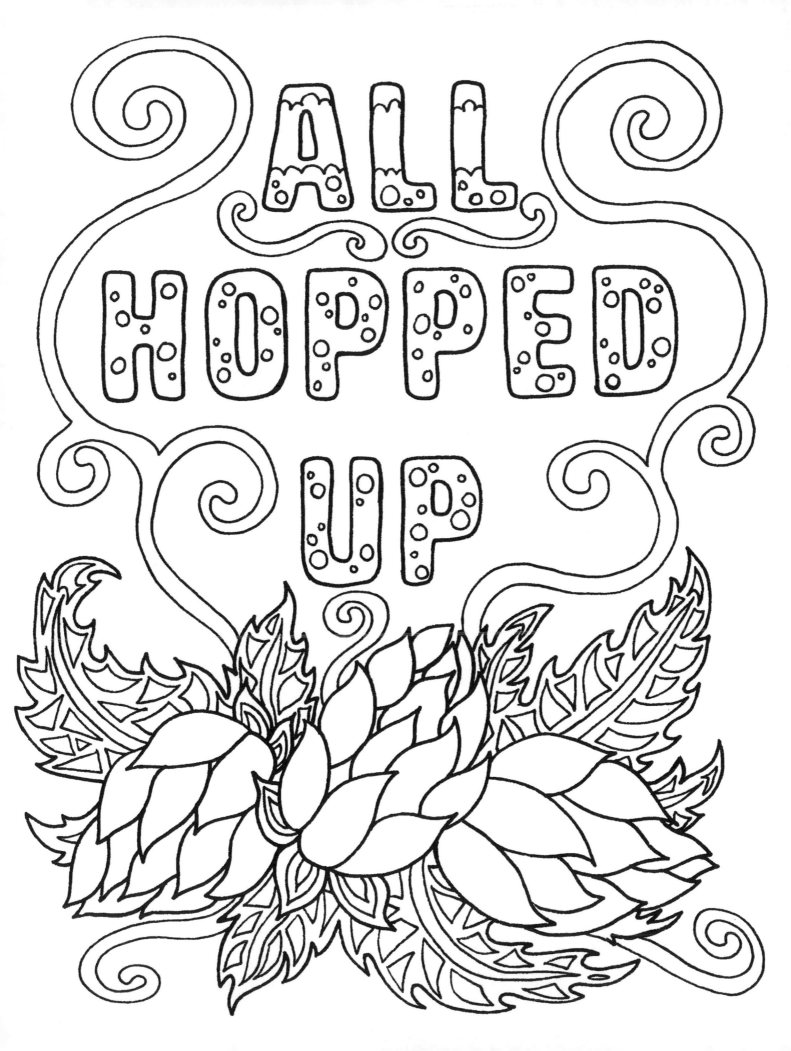

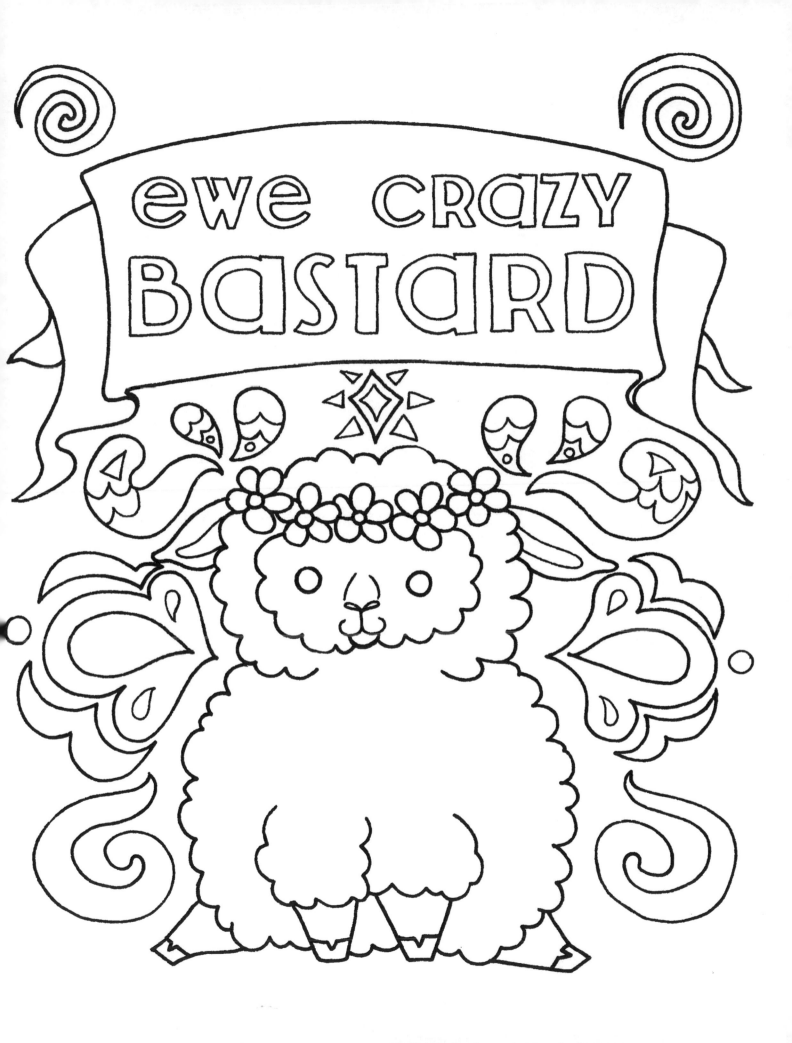

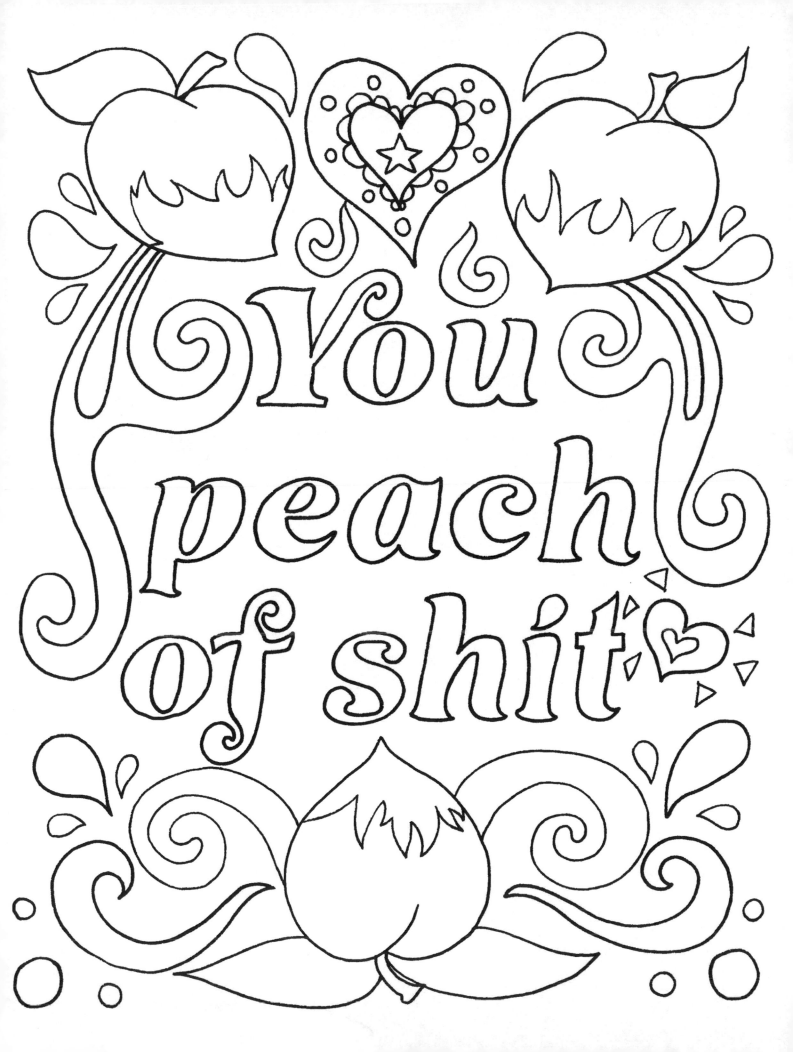

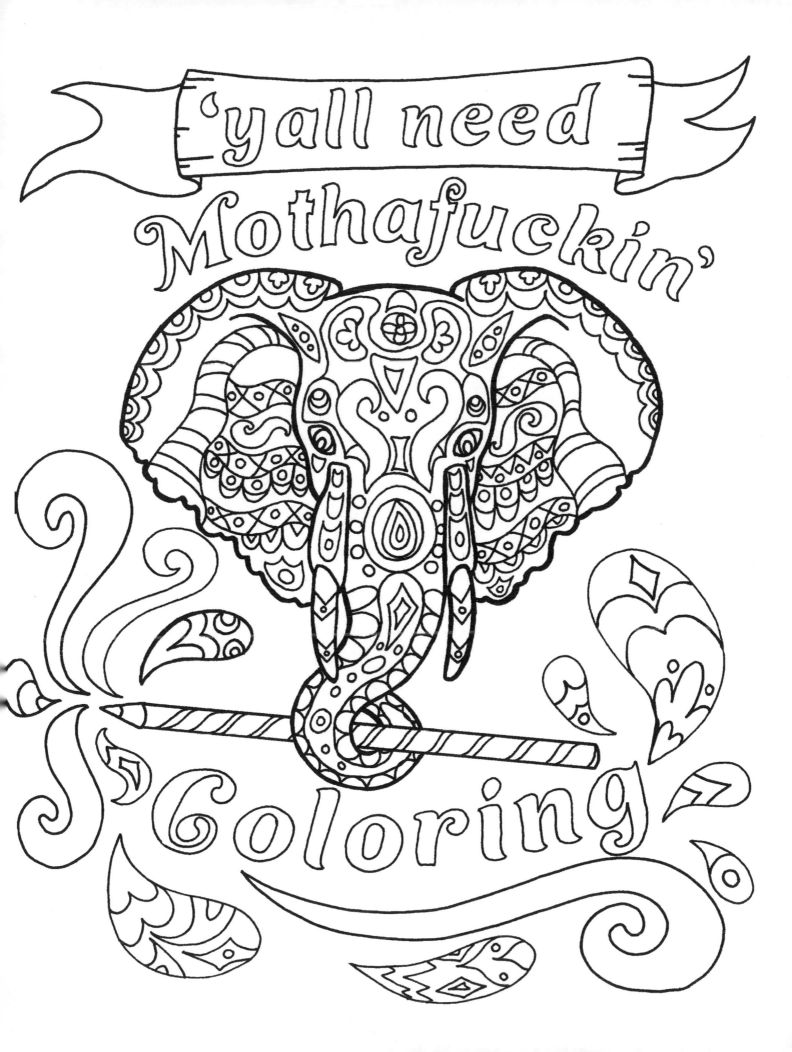

Oh,

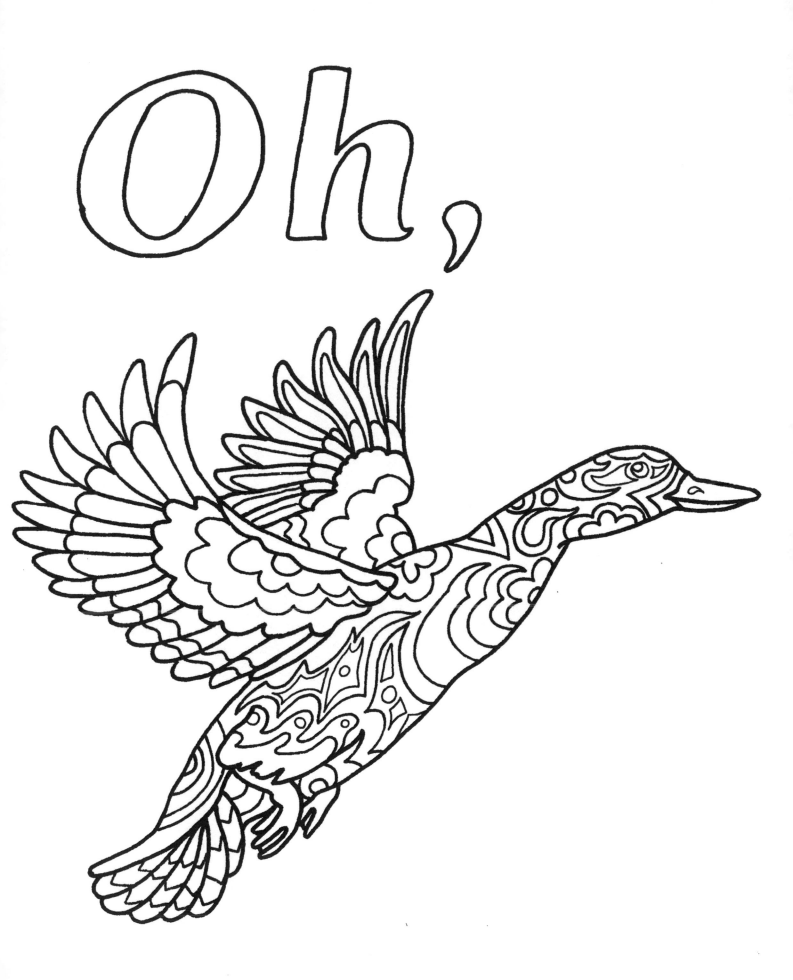

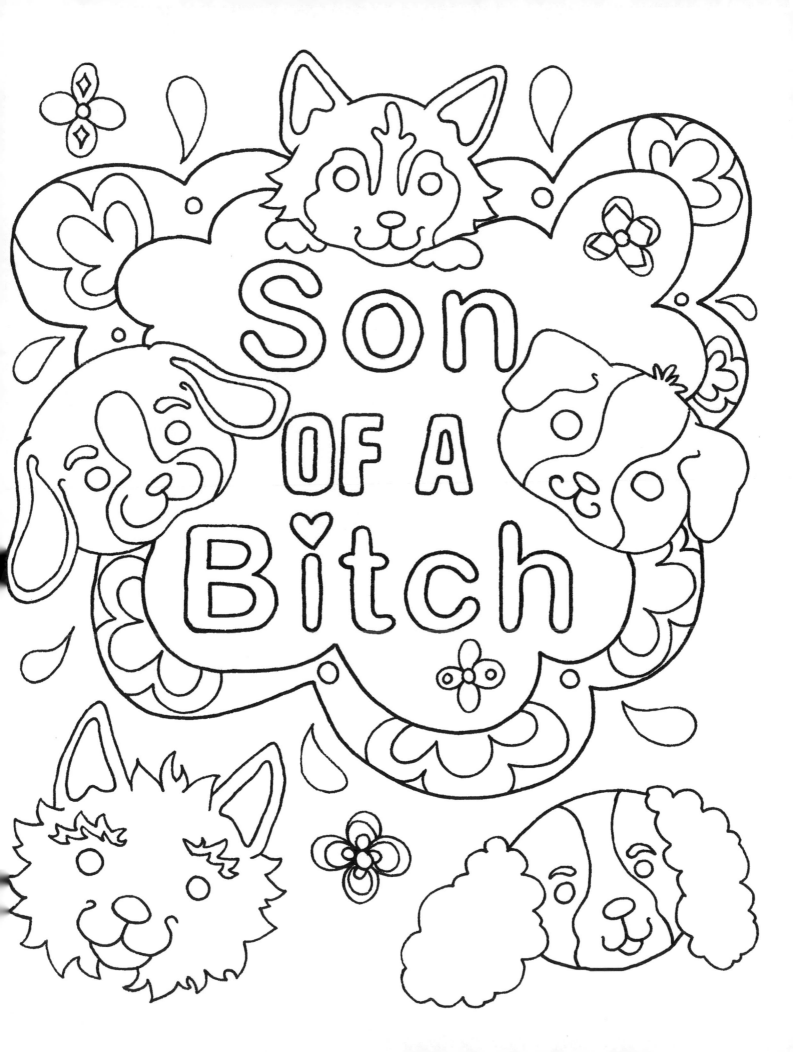

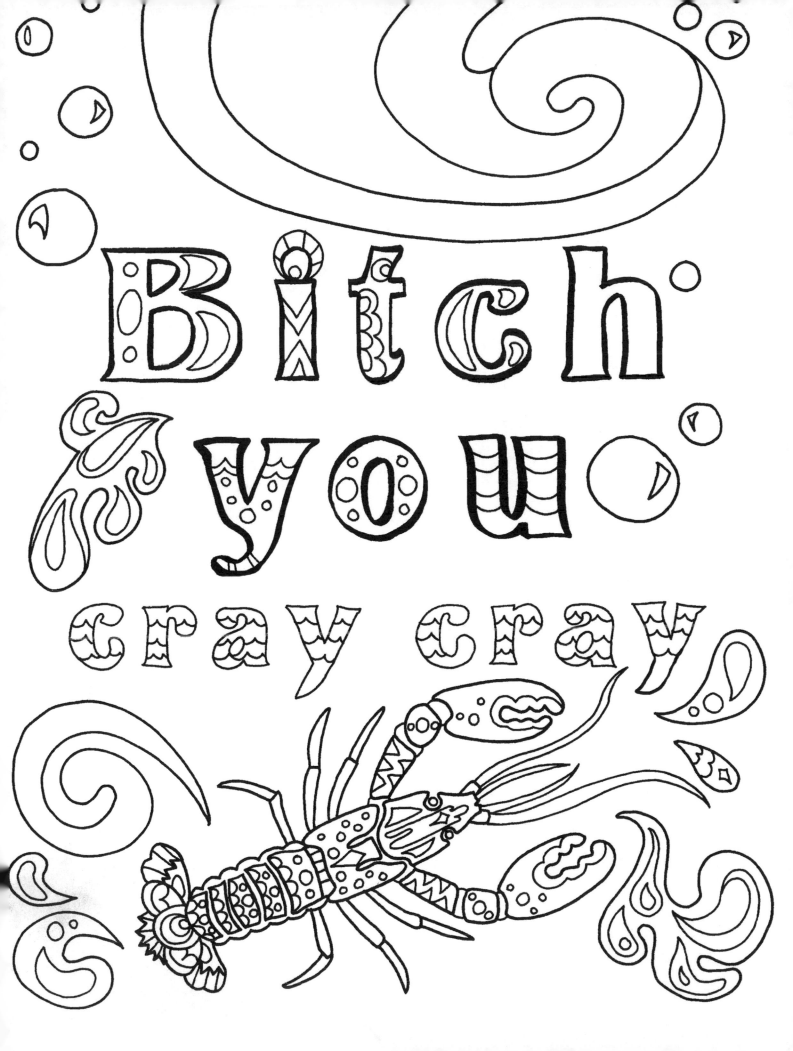

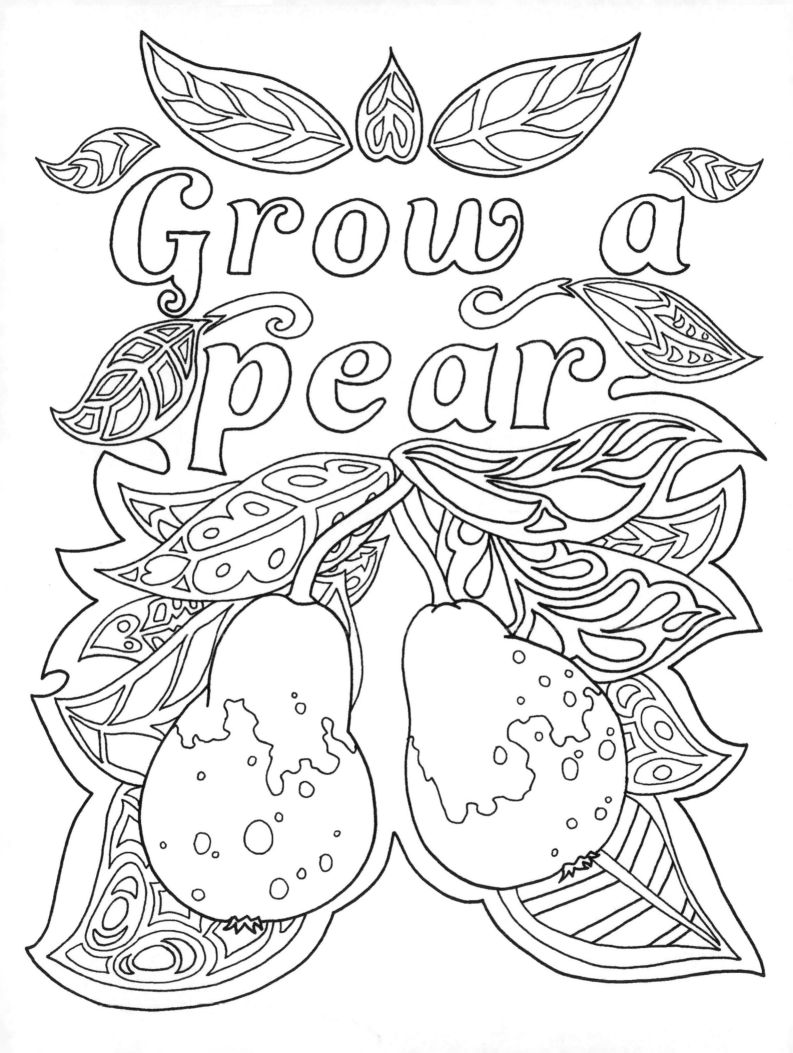

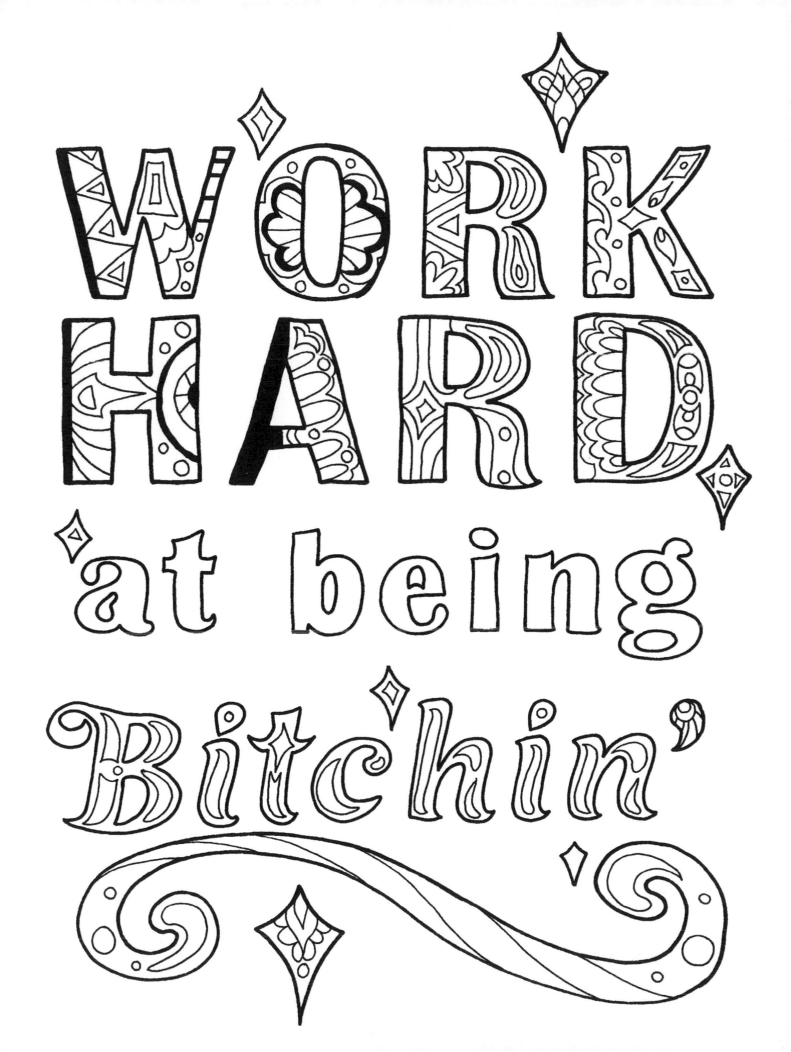

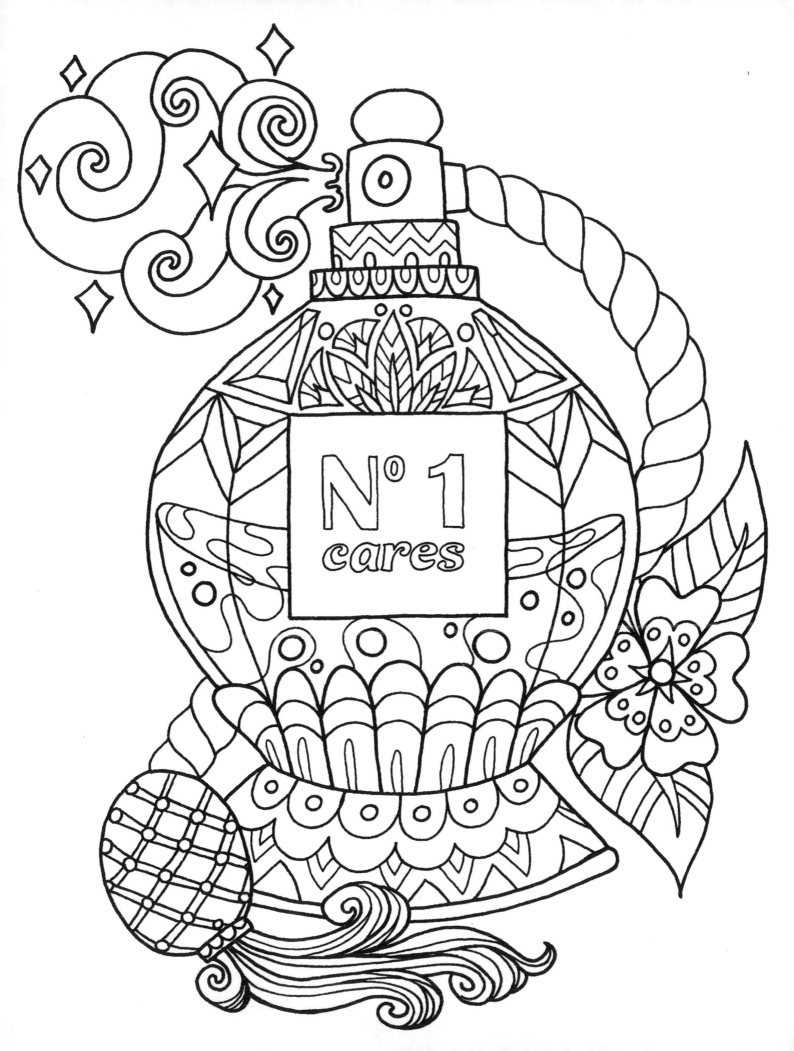

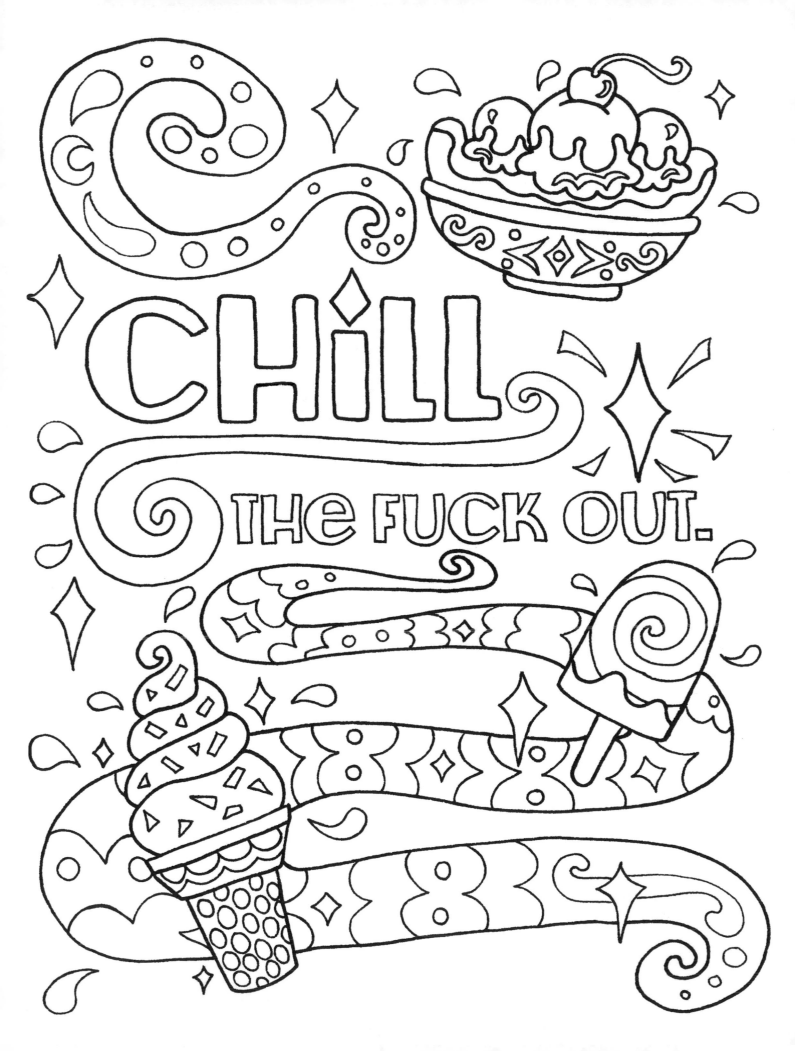

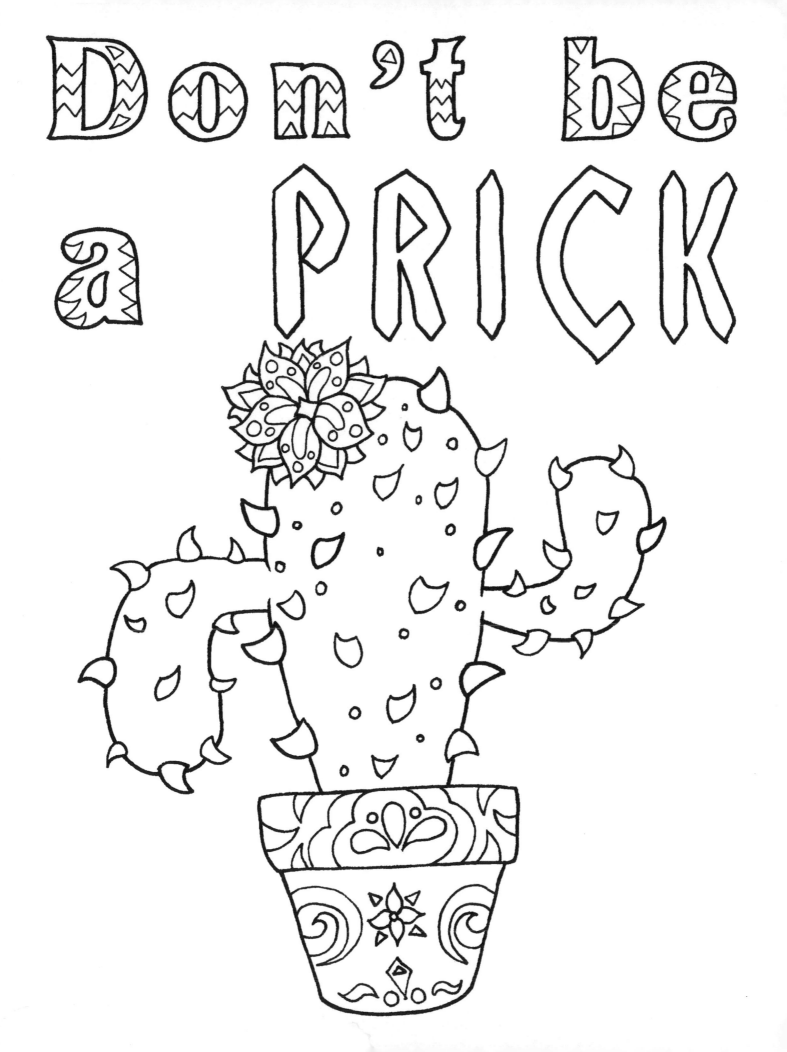

WINE DOWN FOR WHAT

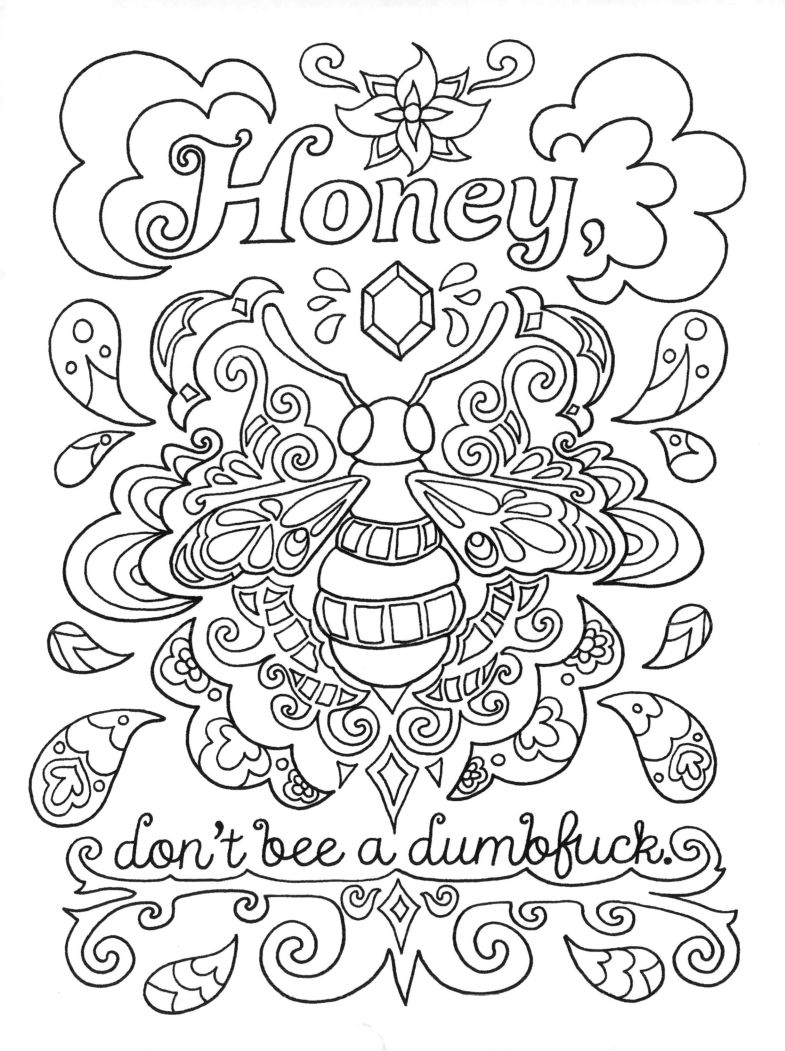

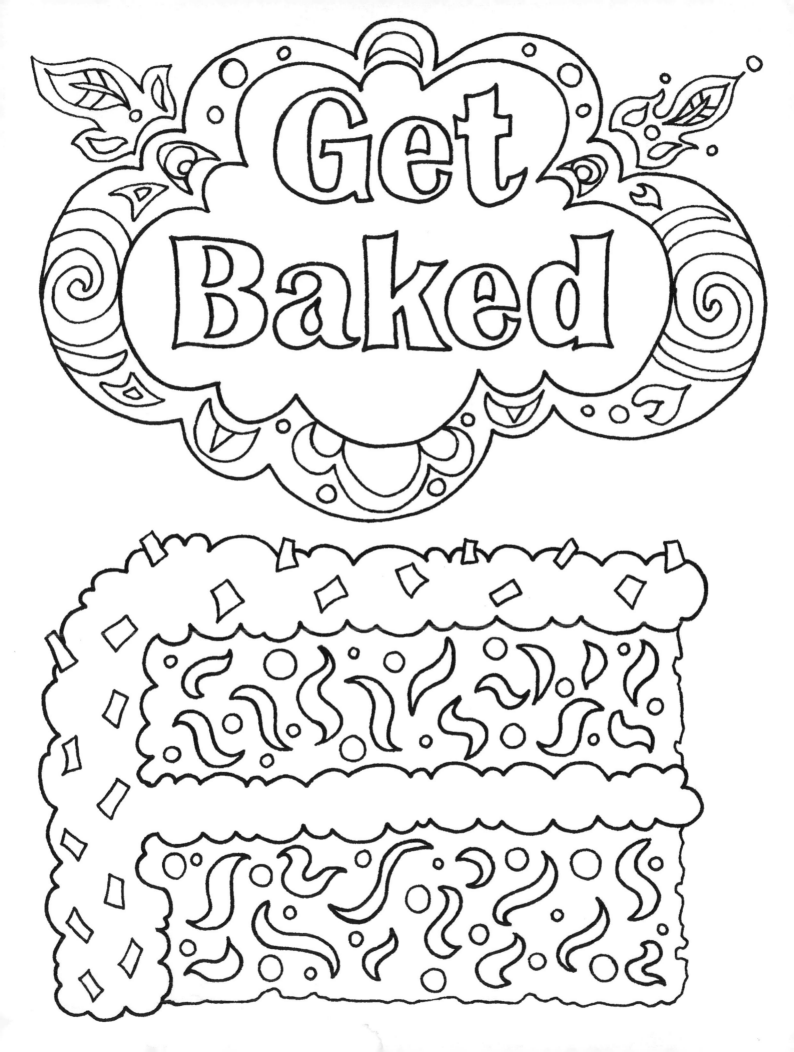

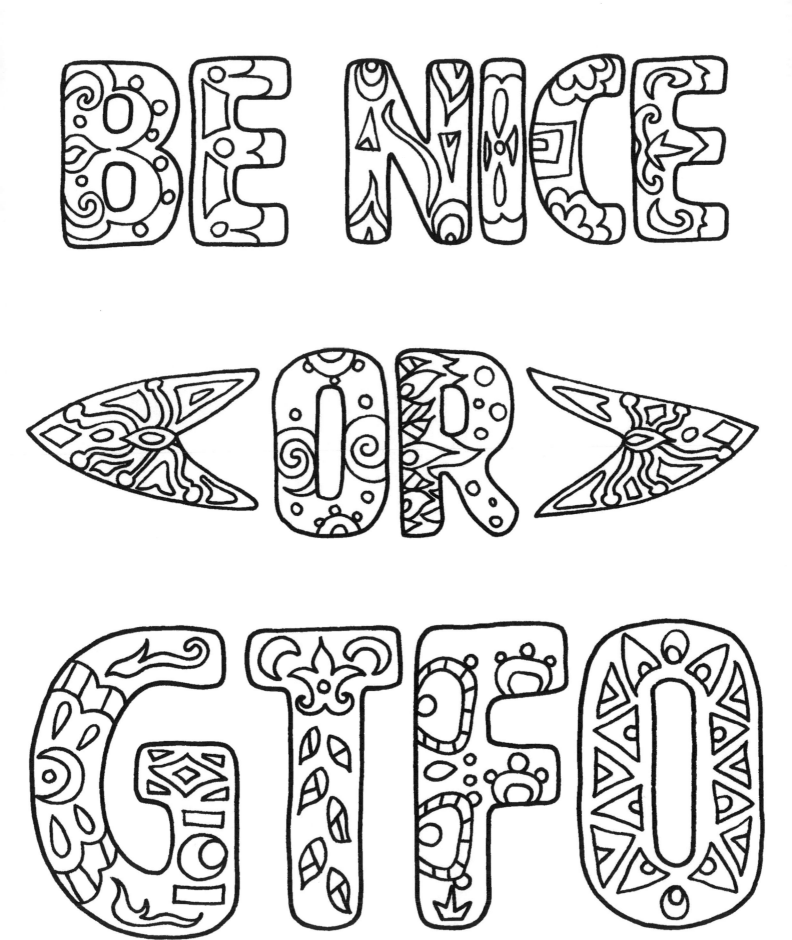

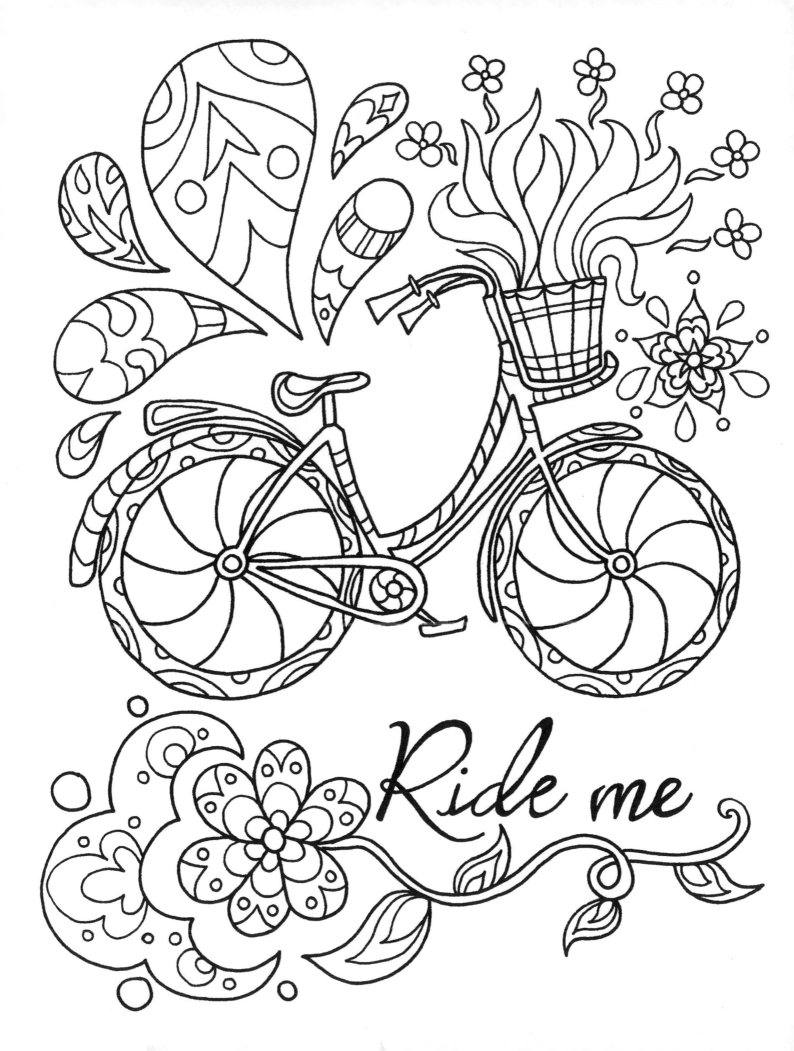

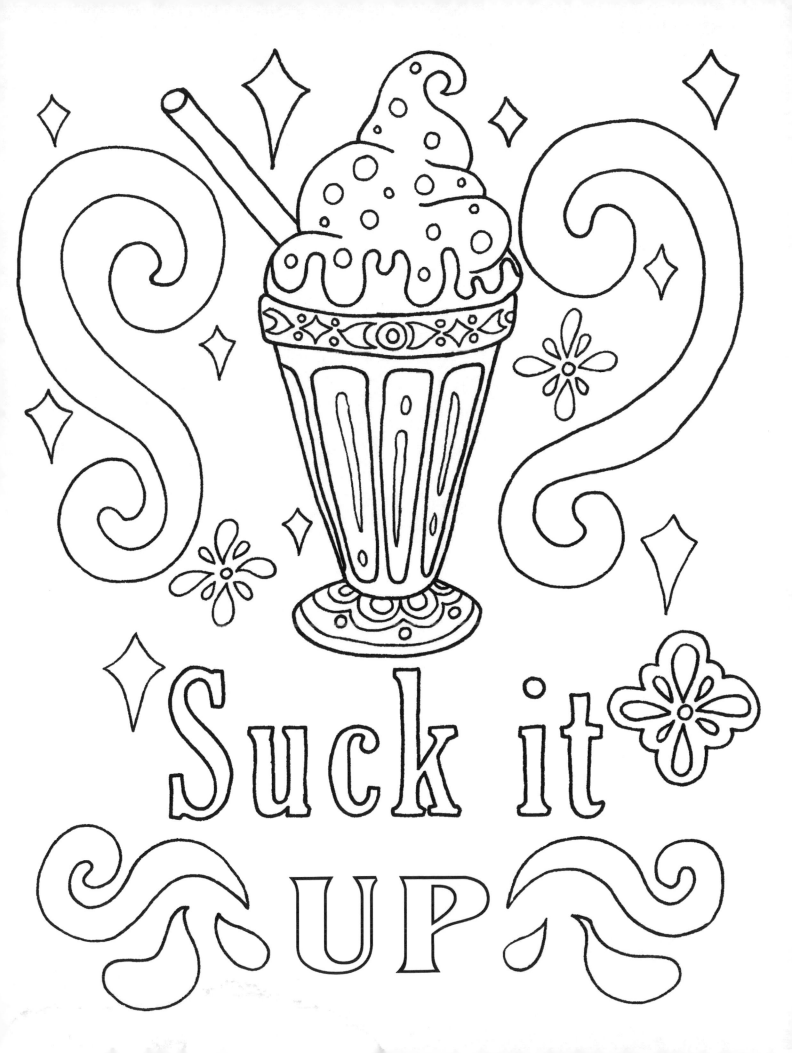

Look at
all the
I Give

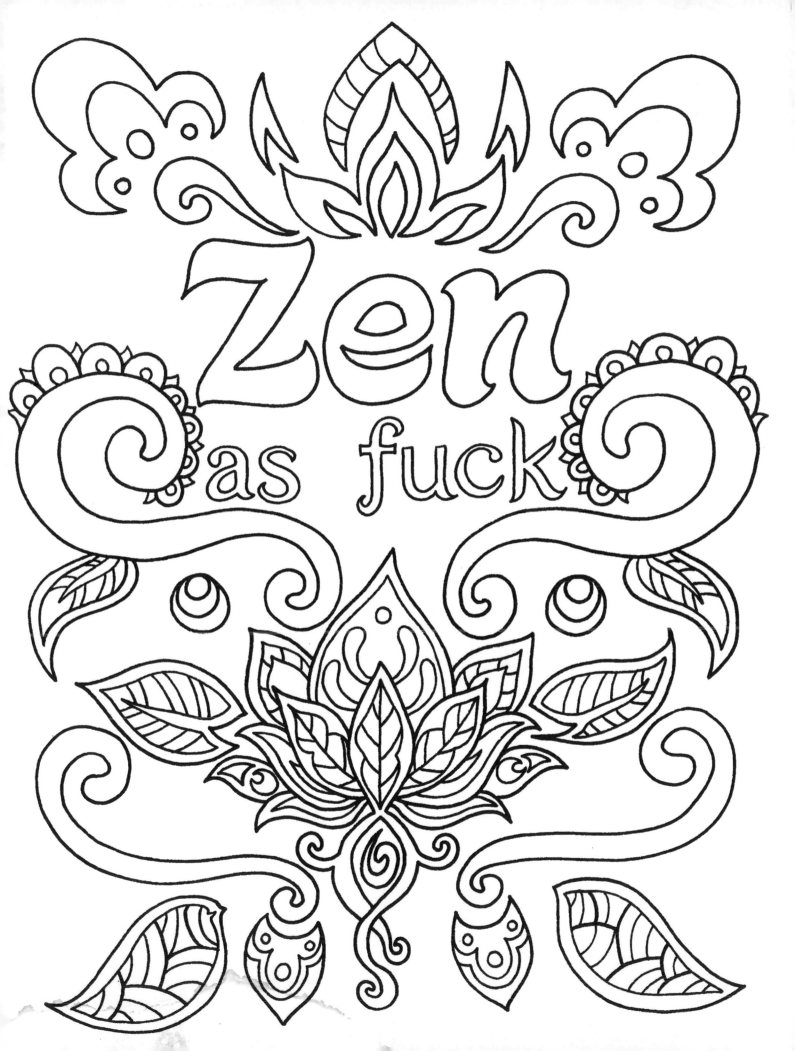

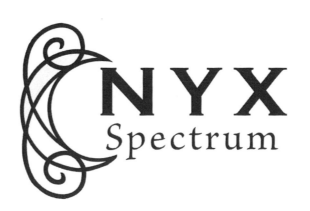